The Amma Parenting Center Book of Sleep

*Using the Sleep Stoplight® to Gently Promote Sleep and Avoid
Cry-It-Out Sleep Training During Your Baby's First Year*

By Sara Pearce RN CNM IBCLC

Copyright 2014 Amma Parenting Center Inc

Contents

Dear Families,

Welcome to *The Amma Parenting Center Book of Sleep: Using the Sleep Stoplight® to Gently Promote Sleep and Avoid Cry-It-Out Sleep Training During Your Baby's First Year*, the sleep education system used by the team at Amma Parenting Center.

As a Registered Nurse, Certified Nurse-Midwife, and International Board Certified Lactation Consultant, I have been working with mothers and babies since 1995. My journey into sleep education began in 2007, when I started Amma Parenting Center with a six-week class for new mothers called the New Mama Class. Every week, I would gather with women whose babies were newborn through two months old, and we would talk about the joys and concerns of new motherhood. While the challenges of parenting are many, I found that the most common questions of new parents were regarding sleep: how to help their babies sleep better, sleep consistently, and sleep longer stretches—so they could sleep, too. Helping parents learn how to set themselves and their babies up for sleep success became one of my specialties.

Over the years, the New Mama program grew, and Amma Parenting Center grew; today, hundreds of women graduate from the New Mama Class every year. Many "Amma Mamas" stay with us in Amma programs throughout their babies' first year, and I keep in touch with them as the years go on. Following families over weeks, months and years has allowed me and my team of teachers to see the long-term outcomes of sleep education. We have found that sleep teaching that starts early, that is done gently and age-appropriately, and that progresses as baby grows has a significant, positive impact on long-term sleep outcomes.

The Sleep Stoplight®, which breaks down the first year of infancy into progressive steps parents can take as their baby develops and gets older, is the teaching tool we use at Amma Parenting Center. The Sleep Stoplight® has become an integral part of the classes offered at Amma for parents in their first year of parenthood.

I didn't do this on my own: Amma's talented team of teachers contributed wisdom, as have two members of our Board of Advisors: Mary Sheedy Kurcinka, D.Ed and Laurel Wills, MD. Research studies and tips and strategies from a range of wise experts have also informed the concepts behind the Sleep Stoplight® (see the bibliography on page 60).

I wish you all the best as you don the superhero cape of Parent. Guiding an infant through his early months is not easy—especially when you're exhausted! But a gentle and compassionate hand and a patient approach will help your baby grow into a secure and connected child. You can do it!

Sincerely,
Sara Pearce, RN CNM IBCLC

AMMA
PARENTING CENTER

About the Sleep Stoplight®

The Sleep Stoplight® *is our age-based sleep education model. These are suggestions—not rules—based on infant development and research. You are the expert on your child, and you get to choose the sleep culture in your family. We respect and honor all the right ways of being a parent and a baby.*

This system was developed in answer to a question we at Amma frequently get about babies and sleep: "When do I have to worry about my baby forming bad sleep habits?"

The answer to the question: Not right away when your baby is a newborn. However, there are helpful steps you can take when your baby is young that will prepare him for good sleep as he grows. During your baby's first year you can "apply the brakes" to behaviors that are unsustainable for your family, but this slow-down needs to happen gradually and in the context of age and of infant development.

The green, yellow, and red stages of the stoplight walk you through what you can do as your baby grows.

Here's what it looks like:

Age	Light	What It Means
Birth to 3 months	Green	Anything goes, as long as it's safe. Set a sleep-friendly environment. Interpret cues and cries. Get to know your baby's personality and preferences. It's important to hold, soothe, and bond. No bad habits form. Your baby is too little to learn independence right now. "Drowsy but awake" can be introduced in the third month. Green means go!
3 to 6 months	Yellow	You can routinely practice more independent sleep. Be consistent with your practice sessions, but end them if baby is stressed. Create sustainable sleep associations and phase out unsustainable ones. Create daily rhythms and rituals by reinforcing emerging patterns. Yellow means slow.
6 to 12 months	Red	Nap schedules and sleep consolidation emerge. If you need to make changes, you can start sleep teaching with love and consistency, taking into account temperament. Keep your base skills going when troubleshooting sleep regressions. Red means whoa.

How To Use the Sleep Stoplight®

Use the Sleep Stoplight® based on your baby's age. When your baby is zero to three months old, just follow the Green Light guidance. You can move to the next stage, or the Yellow Light, at age three to six months; and you can save the Red Light for the second half of his first year.

Don't Skip Ahead

I don't recommend getting a "jump start" on the next stage, because the Sleep Stoplight® is based on infant development and neurologic maturation. Using this kind of age-based approach challenges parents to stay in the moment. This is not always easy. I recognize (and relate to) the exhaustion that can come with parenting a newborn, and the desire to hit a secret fast-forward button to get to the

> **Parent the baby in your arms, not the one in your head.**

sleep-through-the-night age. Learning to parent the baby you have right now and not wishing him to be someone else with better, more advanced abilities is one of the great challenges of parenthood. I call this "parenting the baby in your arms, not the one in your head." It is the bedrock of Amma Parenting Center.

Build Base Skills

Throughout the Sleep Stoplight®, you will be prompted to build and practice what we call "Base Skills." These are the fundamental building blocks that match your baby's age and development. Each stage has its own Base Skills. They are evidence-based essentials for your baby's good sleep. On page 63 you will find a checklist of Base Skills to achieve by your baby's first birthday.

Make It Yours

As you find your voice and values as a parent, your family will have its own unique fingerprint and its own unique approach to the Sleep Stoplight®. The suggestions contained in this book, including Base Skills, can be used in any family, whether you breastfeed or bottle feed, bed share or use a crib, work or stay home. They are relevant to any parenting philosophy. But bottom line, they are only suggestions. You are the expert on your child, and you get to choose the sleep culture in your family; we respect and honor all the right ways of being a parent and a baby. I always tell my New Mamas that part of being a parent is learning to filter advice – even mine!

> **You are the expert on your baby.**

If You're Starting Late, No Problem

If you start our system somewhere in the middle of your baby's first year, don't worry. You can still apply the system. But do read the book from the beginning. Learn and start applying the Base Skills from the previous stages, because you will build on them now and in later stages.

No "System" Can Solve All Problems

Sleep can be hard. Very hard. Children can have a variety of physical issues which impact sleep, and I have seen cases of chronic ear infections, sleep apnea, sensory processing disorders, gastroesophageal reflux disease, and other conditions that prevent good sleep. If you have been working hard and your baby is not making progress or his sleep is getting worse, please see your baby's doctor. There may be physical conditions that need to be addressed before sleep can improve.

I've also seen babies with highly spirited temperaments whose parents do better with throwing out all advice and doing whatever works. Our wise advisor, Mary Sheedy Kurcinka, author of *Raising Your Spirited Child* (William Morrow, 2009), reminds parents of spirited children to aim for "better" instead of "perfect." Well said.

Have Patience and Trust in Yourself and in Your Baby

Think of this system not as a quick fix, but as a long-term teaching endeavor. You're not forcing anything that doesn't come naturally, but rather you are teaching and promoting sleep skills that develop over time. You are the sensei to your little grasshopper. Have patience with your young learner and trust in her abilities. Have confidence in your child, and confidence in yourself.

> Trust your caring instincts.
> The most important outcome is a secure, connected relationship with your child.

Finally, be secure in knowing that YOU are the only expert on your baby and your family. Stay flexible and adaptable, and always rely on your caring instincts. If you try something and sense your baby is not ready, or it doesn't fit with your family, move on and try something else. The most important outcome is not a certain number of hours of sleep by a certain age, but rather a relationship with your baby based on trust, love, and connection.

Start Here, and Read on As Needed

This book is intended to be a short, easy read, and the Sleep Stoplight®
is designed to be intuitive and succinct. Tired families often tell us they
appreciate a summary rather than a thick, academic book with a broad
age range. That said, I've shared wisdom from many sources throughout
the book, and the bibliography contains all of my sources of information
and inspiration. If you're ready to or interested in reading in depth on a
particular topic or strategy, then the bibliography is your starting point.

A Gentle Reminder about Your Little Primate

It helps to remember that human beings are animals, and primates at
that. We have evolved over millennia to survive and perpetuate our
species, and many of the bodily characteristics and behaviors your
newborn exhibits reflect ancient hardwiring for adaptation.

Reflexes that don't seem to make sense become logical when put in
context. The stepping reflex, whereby a newborn baby bends his knee
and then straightens his leg, as if taking a step, seems out of place when
you consider that he won't walk for another year. But when placed
on his tummy on his mama's chest after birth, this stepping reflex helps
propel him up towards the breast, and his little feet perform abdominal
massage on Mom, triggering the uterine contractions that prevent
excess maternal blood loss.

Studying tribal cultures and indigenous peoples sheds light on infant
behavior. It is the biological norm in hunter-gatherer societies for infants
to be held almost continuously, never separated from their mothers and
nursing often. This is the default state of almost every newborn primate
infant: staying in the "natural habitat" of mama's arms, in a semi-
upright prone position, nursing frequently. Infants in traditional human
societies (and baby great apes) continue this close contact at night,
never sleeping alone. Staying close to Mama, well-nourished and well-
protected, is what helps human infants avoid predators, grow up safe
and strong, and go on to have more humans.

Of course, I know your baby is not a tiny orangutan, nor are you likely a member of an African, New Guinean or Amazonian traditional society. But that doesn't make your baby any more aware that he's in the 21st century, where he is expected to sleep alone, nurse on a schedule, and go 12 hours without you at a young age.

So when you're perplexed at your newborn's low threshold for independence, her seeking you out in the middle of the night, her frequent eating and her love of the "natural habitat" of your softly rising and falling chest enveloped in your loving arms, remember: she is only primate, after all.

AMMA
PARENTING CENTER

green light sleep

When baby is 0-3 months old: Green means go!
Anything goes, as long as it's safe.

In A Nutshell
Create a sleep-friendly environment. Interpret cues and cries. Get to know your baby's personality and preferences. It's important to hold, soothe, establish feeding, and bond. No bad habits form. Your baby is too little to learn independence right now. If your baby is ready, start introducing the concept of "drowsy but awake" when being put down in the third month.

The Three Base Skills You'll Learn in the Green Light Stage
- Create a sleep-friendly environment (page 21).
- Interpret cues and cries (page 22).
- Introduce "drowsy but awake" in the third month (page 25).

Up Next in the Yellow Light Stage
- Practice more sleep independence.
- Support emerging patterns.
- Work with sleep associations.

Overview of the Green Light Stage

When your baby is a newborn, it's important to respond to all her needs and set up a foundation of trust and connection. The Green Light stage is all about everybody in the family getting as much sleep as possible while establishing feeding, recovering from childbirth, and settling into your new life. Newborn babies need a lot of sleep (and can't learn bad habits at this age), and new mothers need rest and sleep for physical and emotional wellbeing.

Have Realistic Expectations about Sleep

Our cultural attitudes about sleep are sometimes at odds with our babies' biology and abilities. The pressure to get a baby to sleep longer and better and through the night can be stressful and unrealistic. Recognize that what your culture wants your baby to do (indeed, even what YOU want your baby to do) might not fit with her capabilities right now. Slow down to your baby's pace and try to spend time in the moment. Resist the urge to worry about bad habits. Sleep education is a marathon, not a sprint.

> **The biological norm for human infants is to be in close physical proximity to their parents.**

The bedrock of a human baby's biology is the drive for connection with his or her parents. They are wired in every way to be close to you, and will sound an alarm if they need food, care, or comfort. This is biologically normal behavior for infants! **Soothe, hold, and bond with your baby.** There is a beautiful series of interwoven physical responses when a baby is held safe and secure in your arms, and this leads to better sleep. Follow your caring instincts and trust that all of this connection and contact is just right for your baby now.

Understand the Science of Sleep

Newborn babies need an average of 16-18 hours of sleep per day. This number can be greatly variable, and it's important to recognize this wide range of normal.

In the newborn months, babies sleep in 30 to 45-minute cycles that can repeat several times during a nap or night. Infant sleep is either "quiet" (the baby version of non-REM sleep) or "active" (the baby version of REM sleep). Active sleep is important for brain development and for SIDS prevention, but it is lighter and more restless. Most sleep is active sleep at this age. Experts believe that all this light sleep is *bio-protective* for newborns, or good for their health—because the increased alertness guards against SIDS, and because all of the overnight eating keeps mother's milk at a high rate of production. Quiet sleep increases around four months, after which the rate of SIDS incidences start to fall. See how perfectly engineered your baby is?

> The American Academy of Pediatrics wants parents to remember how important and protective light sleep is to infants. In *Sleep: What Every Parent Needs to Know* (AAP, 2013) they write: "A good sleeper is a child who wakes up frequently but can get himself back to sleep. It is not a child who sleeps without waking for 10 hours a night. Frequent waking is developmentally appropriate and allows the baby to wake up when he is in a situation in which he is not getting enough oxygen or is having problems breathing. Sleeping undisturbed for prolonged periods at this age is not healthy."

Because active sleep comes first in the sleep cycle, your baby will sleep lightly in the first 20 minutes after falling asleep. Trying to put your sleeping baby down so you can get things done may be more successful if you wait until you see signs of quiet sleep: fewer body movements and twitches, deeper and more regular breathing, and eyes not moving under the eyelids. Once your baby has entered quiet sleep, she won't wake up as easily and may transition out of your arms without waking up. Wearing your baby in a carrier frees up your hands while supporting your baby for sleep and fulfilling her biological need for closeness to you.

> **Your baby will start sleep in an Active Sleep state and transition to Quiet Sleep after about 20 minutes.**

Changing from one sleep cycle to the next can bring about a very light sleep, or even a temporary wake-up. I call this a "Fake Wake." If your baby has only been sleeping for a short time (20-30 minutes) and starts to rouse, wait a few moments to see if she will fall back to sleep spontaneously. Many times babies will appear to be waking up, when in fact it's only a few moments of pseudo-wakefulness between sleep cycles. Of course, if it's been a while since her last feeding session, there's no need to wait too long. She may give early hunger cues like bringing her hands to her mouth, rooting, and smacking her lips – all of which tell you it's time to eat again. Newborns need frequent and unrestricted feeding sessions at the breast so that nursing has a successful start.

Day-night reversal is common for newborns. This is largely a function of brain maturation, and resolves in time. Keeping the sleeping environment very dark at night and exposing your baby to early morning daylight (even through a window) upon waking will help support the development of circadian rhythms. Breastfeeding, infant massage, and skin-to-skin contact have all been shown to promote brain maturation.

Understand How Feeding Impacts Sleep

Newborns have small stomachs, and need to eat frequently throughout the day and night to keep up with their tremendously fast rate of growth. Overnight feeding is the norm for both breastfed and formula-fed babies for many months to come. Some babies have smaller stomach capacities than others and will need to snack frequently, up to 14 or more times a day. Other babies can eat as little as eight times a day. Mothers have different milk storage capacities in their breasts (and you can't tell by bra cup size).

Each mother-baby pair is unique, and feeding patterns will affect sleep patterns. Trust your newborn to lead the way in regards to her feeding needs, and respond whenever she asks. In the early weeks of breastfeeding, milk supply capacity is being established. As a lactation consultant, I want you to nurse your baby frequently and upon request, even overnight, knowing that the work you're doing now will pay off for the whole duration of breastfeeding.

The majority of newborns have some degree of acid reflux, whereby the valve which seals the entrance to the stomach is weak and lets milk regurgitate back up into the esophagus. This can manifest itself in different ways (not all of which results in spitting up), and the management is small frequent meals, holding straight upright after a meal, and patience. According to the American Academy of Pediatrics, elevating the head of the crib for sleep has not been proven to help. Only the most significant cases are treated with medicine. Most babies will fare well, gain weight and be relatively content.

If your baby does have significant acid reflux she may need smaller, more frequent feedings and may be more uncomfortable, which will impact how long she can sleep. This will usually improve greatly after 4 to 6 months.

Anticipate "The Fussies"

It's common for babies to start off sleepy, become more wakeful at 2-3 weeks, and be increasingly fussy until about 6 to 8 weeks. I call this age "The Fussies." I love Harvey Karp's *The Happiest Baby on the Block* (Bantam, 2008); Dr. Karp's "5 Ss" (swaddling, side/stomach positioning, shushing sounds, swinging, and sucking) have greatly helped many parents.

Your baby needs you for soothing and comforting because he is still developing the ability to soothe himself. It's very common for newborns to sleep for hours in your loving arms, but for only a short time when alone in a crib. Babies are wired to view separation from a parent as abnormal, and will seek you out when they do not feel emotionally or physically at peace. Now is the time to invest in a comfortable sling, wrap or baby carrier, because if your goal is to foster independence in a newborn, you will surely lose that battle.

Most babies at this age fuss, cry, and cluster feed more in the late afternoon and early evening. Sometimes parents perceive this as a sleep problem or a feeding problem, but in most cases it's just normal newborn behavior. Maternal sleep hormones are concentrated in breast milk in higher levels as the day goes on, so cluster nursing in the evening helps your baby sleep better at night. Breastfed babies will suckle and nurse for comfort, and many moms quickly figure out that breastfeeding is a secret weapon in the war against fussing!

Remember that Your Baby is a Unique Individual

It's impossible to talk about sleep as a "one size fits all" experience. Babies are just tiny people, and they come with the same sleep preferences and sensitivities that grownups have. Be a student of your baby: Does she get hot easily? Does she sleep better in a really dark room? How sensitive is she to noise? How fast does she ramp up from mildly tired to exhausted? Be aware of advice that doesn't seem to fit with your child. Only *you* are the expert on *your* baby.

How much your baby sleeps is a reflection of their development, personality, feeding needs, and environment. Do what you can to promote sleep, but remember that your baby is in control right now.

Honor Your Own Unique Qualities (and Needs!), Too

You are a unique individual as well! Your own temperament affects the way you parent. It also affects the way you respond to change, challenges, and sleep deprivation. Awareness of your own responses and needs will help you understand the dynamics happening in your new family. Your own upbringing and the culture in which you were raised will also impact your style. If this is your first child, know that you are doing a lot of learning right now, so have patience with yourself. This is the biggest job you'll have with no training beforehand.

Sleep Location

The ideal location for your baby at night is close to you and in a safe sleep environment. The pediatrician editor of the AAP sleep book, *Sleep: What Every Parent Needs to Know*, recommends that babies sleep in their parent's room for the first 6 to 12 months of life to reduce the risk of SIDS. Many parents love the bassinets that connect to the bed like a sidecar. These are terrific for facilitating breastfeeding and responding to your baby's needs without placing her in a potentially unsafe sleeping environment.

If, after doing your research, you feel that bed sharing is the best fit for your family, the key is to do it with intention and to make it safe. Rules for safe bed sharing are easily found online or in *The Happiest Baby Guide to Great Sleep* by Harvey Karp (William Morrow, 2013). I just want to make sure you are taking *deliberate steps* to ensure safety and not bringing the baby into bed with you (or falling asleep together on a couch or recliner) out of exhaustion and desperation while you're half asleep and have impaired judgment.

Although you may be tired enough to let it happen, *do not fall asleep while holding your baby*. It puts your baby at risk of smothering

> **If you decide to sleep with your baby in your bed, do it with intention and make it safe.**

or entrapment, either in your arms or in the furniture, and is highly dangerous. If your baby sleeps better while close to you, it is safer to create a close-but-separate location (like a bassinet, co-sleeper or swing next to your bed) or actually share your bed with your baby with the right safety precautions.

Remember the rules for SIDS prevention in all sleep environments: have the baby share your room, keep the room temperature cool, put baby on her back, and clear all bedding and objects—including bumpers—out of the crib or bassinet. Do not expose your baby to secondhand smoke, and keep up with vaccinations. Exclusively breastfed babies have only a quarter of the SIDS risk as babies who exclusively drink formula. Babies who drink even some breast milk have half the SIDS risk.

Sleeping in "Containers"

The American Academy of Pediatrics recommends against "sitting devices" for routine sleep. The reason is that infants, especially those under 4 months, may end up in upright positions that compromise their ability to breathe. The AAP defines these devices as "car safety seats, strollers, infant carriers, and infant slings."

This caution is necessary, and you must be vigilant about your baby's airway at all times. Some sitting devices can keep your baby in too much of an upright angle, causing his chin to flex down onto his chest. Tight flexion may cause his airway to be too constricted. Many newborns truly do sleep better with motion or in a semi-upright position, so if your baby falls asleep in a sling, swing or bouncy seat, remember the guidance below.

Do not use the car seat for a bed. Car safety seats have rocker bottoms that can cause the angle to be too upright or unstable. (This is not a concern when infant car seats are snapped into their bases and the angle is correct.) If your baby falls asleep in the car seat and you bring him into the house after returning home, either move him to the crib or keep a close eye on him.

Carefully position your baby in slings and wraps in a semi-upright position to ensure his chin is not tightly flexed, and keep fabric away from his face – you must be able to see your baby's face at all times. Fully recline swing seats. You always want to be able to fit a couple of fingers between your baby's chin and his chest.

Make sure your baby's head, neck, and spine are aligned to prevent his head from tilting or twisting to one side for too long while sleeping in a "container." You can do this by putting rolled burp cloths or receiving blankets on either side of your baby's head and making sure his hips are straight. Torticollis is a condition in which the neck muscles are tight on one side, resulting in a persistent head tilt or twist. In most cases it's present from birth, but can develop or worsen when a baby defaults into the tilt or twist all the time and their full range of motion isn't developed.

Babies need plenty of time to move their heads and necks freely with no pressure on the back of the head. Tummy time should be offered frequently throughout the day. When your baby is bobbling his head about, he's developing important head and neck control and range of motion.

The First Green Light Base Skill: Create a Sleep-Friendly Environment

Knowing what makes a successful sleep environment is a Base Skill of the Green Light stage. Here, I will teach you how to create an environment that is conducive to successful sleep for your baby.

Right from the start, create a "sleep-friendly" environment at night. Keep the room very dark with minimal or no artificial light (including night lights). It should be dark enough that you cannot read a book without turning on a light. Exposure to the right light levels at the right time of day have been shown to promote the development of circadian rhythms.

For tasks like feeding or diaper changing, use a low-wattage red night light. Red light wavelengths have been shown to disrupt melatonin secretion the least. White (or blue) wavelengths are known to be disruptive to sleep hormones. If you spend time in front of screens (TV, tablets, or smart phones) in the middle of the night, you might consider turning those off so *you* get better sleep, too.

Expose your baby to plenty of daylight when awake during the day, especially in the morning. Full-spectrum daylight supports the hormonal cues for wakefulness.

White noise from a high-quality white noise machine can help greatly with sleep. I recommend buying a good product designed to last, instead of a phone or computer with a white noise app or a stuffed animal that has a timer. Continuous white noise machines should not be louder than 50 decibels, and should be placed at least 6 feet from the baby's sleeping location in order to stay within safe noise levels. Eventually, when your baby is sleeping in her room for nights and naps, you will use that white noise machine to both promote and cue sleep.

A cool room is conducive to sleep and is part of the recommendations for SIDS reduction. In the summer months, if you do not use air conditioning, then use a fan and dress your baby in light sleepwear to keep her cool.

At some point your baby may lose the ability to sleep in a stimulating environment during the day; I often see babies lose this adaptability around 6 to 8 weeks. You may find it helpful to use a sleep-friendly room for daytime naps when you see this change. If your baby is able to sleep well despite bright lights and noise, there's no need to change anything.

In summary, a night-time sleep-friendly environment:

- is very dark with no blue or white night light.
- has a red night light for caregiving tasks.
- has a white noise machine.
- is cool.
- has minimal distractions.
- ends in the morning with exposure to morning daylight.

The Second Green Light Base Skill: Interpret Cues and Cries

When it comes to eating and sleeping, I have a saying: Cues, not clocks. This means that you should let the baby decide when to sleep, and offer a nap or bedtime when your baby's body needs it, versus an arbitrary time on the clock. Schedules are not recommended at this stage. Reading your baby's sleep cues is another important Base Skill. Now I'll teach you to use your eyes and ears for information about your baby's needs, and how the right cue reading can help you parent for sleep.

> **Cues, not clocks**

Visual Cues: What Do You See?

As your baby becomes sleepy, cues advance from subtle to overt. I break these down into three stages. Let's look at them in order (knowing, of course, that in reality babies are sometimes not orderly and linear!).

- Sneaky Signs: Staring, looking away, stilling of body movements, and redness around the eyes are all the earliest signs of drowsiness. Your baby may disengage from you and her environment by appearing uninterested or very quiet. At Amma, these early signs have earned the nickname the "Golden Moment," because if you catch it in time, it's the most successful time to offer sleep to a baby.

- Obvious Signs: Yawning, eye rubbing, droopy eyelids, and fussing are often next. These are signs anyone, including a babysitter, would correctly interpret as fatigue. If you see these, it means you may have missed an earlier set of cues.

- You Missed It: Crying, screeching or screaming, big body movements like flailing of arms or kicking of feet, head shaking, arching the back, and face raking are potential signs that your baby is overtired. Sometimes this will look like your baby is getting a second wind of energy after a spell of drowsiness. It may look like your baby is hyper or keyed up, or fighting sleep. These cues mean your baby is *overtired*.

When you see early drowsy cues, offer sleep. This means doing whatever helps your baby fall asleep (nurse, swaddle, rock, snuggle, put him in a baby carrier or in his crib, etc.). If your baby needs additional help falling asleep during daylight hours, try moving into the dark, sleep-friendly environment with the white noise machine.

During the day, most newborns will start showing sleep cues *within 45 to 120 minutes of waking up* from the last sleep session. Be aware of this need for frequent naps and keep an eye out for cues. The same rule applies overnight: If you have a night owl, she will rarely be awake for more than one to two hours without showing drowsy cues. Once day-night reversal has corrected itself, your baby's wakefulness at night will usually be much shorter.

Some babies give obvious cues with plenty of time for their parents to react. Other babies give off quick, subtle cues that are harder to notice and escalate rapidly. If your baby is a tricky cue-giver, be assured that your interpretation skills will get better and better as you learn more about your baby.

> **Offer sleep at the earliest signs of drowsiness, usually seen 45 to 120 minutes after waking up.**

Auditory Cues: What Do You Hear?

Learning to read your baby's cries and noises is another important skill. While transitioning from one sleep cycle to the next (or from active to quiet sleep), your baby may whimper, cry out, or even open her eyes. As described earlier, this is what I call a "fake wake." See where the noises are going: Are they winding down, or are they escalating? If you wait a few moments, you may find the cries lessen and fade, and the baby goes back into quiet sleep.

Getting your baby up at the first peep may interrupt the transition to another sleep cycle, resulting in a shorter sleep episode than your baby needed. This can lead to overtired and dysfunctional sleep. Listen for the "come get me" cry so that you know your baby is truly awake.

Of course, if your baby has been sleeping for a while and hasn't eaten in several hours, you do not need to wait until your baby cries. Go to your hungry baby as she's waking up so that she doesn't get frantically hungry.

Preventing Overtired

When babies get overtired, their bodies produce a stress hormone called cortisol, which can result in shorter or more restless sleep, and which tends to last for a long time in the body (its half-life is about 1 to 2 hours). This is why keeping a baby awake in the hopes of improving sleep rarely works, and helping your baby avoid becoming overtired improves overall sleep. Dr. Marc Weisbluth (*Healthy Sleep Habits, Happy Child*, 1999) coined the phrase "sleep begets sleep." A well-rested baby sleeps better at the next sleep episode.

If your baby has reached the overtired stage and is having a hard time falling asleep, then have patience and do what you can to help your baby sleep. Holding, rocking, taking a car ride, loud white noise, and a very dark room can help. Once your baby gets a good nap, hopefully he will reboot (I call this "hitting control-alt-delete") and will do better with the next sleep episode. If he gets very overtired, you may struggle through a few rough sleep episodes. Do the best you can and eventually your baby will return to her baseline. Very careful cue reading and a successful environment can help.

Young babies often need help falling asleep and staying asleep. You may notice better and longer naps when you are holding her or using a gentle motion. This is all normal, age-appropriate behavior. Independence, especially with sleep, takes a long time to develop. I promise that it gets better with time!

The Third Green Light Base Skill: Introduce "Drowsy but Awake" in the Third Month

The American Academy of Pediatrics recommends starting the habit of putting babies down to sleep in their cribs while they are "drowsy but awake" from Day One. This means being watchful for early signs of drowsiness, soothing and preparing her for sleep as appropriate, and then putting her in her sleep location *while still aware of her surroundings*. Even if it's only for the briefest of moments before falling asleep, your baby will grow accustomed to the feelings and sensations of being in the bed at the time of sleep. Over time, this reduces the chances that the baby will become dependent on being held all the time for sleep.

This skill may be easier said than done. Many young infants have a high need for contact, and may not nap well out of your arms, which is why I recommend waiting until the third month (after 8 weeks or so). Breastfed babies are famous for falling asleep at the breast, and who can blame them? It's so warm and snuggly there! Don't worry. If you practice "drowsy but awake" but are met with resistance, or if it makes sleep significantly worse, just wait and try again in a week or two. It will get better with time. Most babies aren't ready to start this until after The Fussies are over, while some babies aren't ready to be put down for sleep until well into the Yellow Light

> Introduce "drowsy but awake" after The Fussies are over.

zone (age 3 to 6 months). The important thing is to keep "drowsy but awake" on your radar and don't wait too long to start practicing.

Self Care

The Green Light stage is all about patience. Very young babies simply need time to mature and develop. I know that the dishes are driving you bananas and that your friend's baby slept through the night at five weeks (or so she says). Embrace *your* reality and slow down to your baby's pace. In the meantime, tend to your own physical and emotional needs so you have the stamina to endure these sleepless weeks.

Does everyone tell you to sleep when the baby sleeps? This well-meaning advice can be unsuccessful for some new parents. Between the daylight, the phone ringing, the household chores and all the other distractions, it can be difficult to fall asleep in the middle of the day (and then you can get anxious and stressed about your inability to fall asleep). Naps are great if you can get them, but read on for other tips.

If you are parenting with a partner, take shifts. Split the night into two halves, so you can front-load your night with some solid sleep. Go to bed (in a very dark room, with your phone off and no other distractions) at around 8 or 9 pm. Wake only to feed the baby, and then hand her off to your partner for diapering and burping, and go right back to sleep. Switch at 1 am so it's your turn to tend to the baby whenever she wakes up, and allow your partner to sleep undisturbed.

When you do get to sleep, sleep in. Way in. If you need eight hours of sleep to function, make your "night" as long as needed in order to get to that eighth hour. Don't get out of your pajamas; don't get up to check email. Just keep going right back to bed after feeding and caring for your baby until you are caught up. It's ok if this takes until 2 pm.

Simplify your life. Recognize that you are currently in what may be the hardest weeks of your baby's first year. You deserve to slow down, and take time for yourself. There's no reason to fold clean laundry—just leave it in the laundry basket and pick out what you need for the day.

When faced with the list of tasks you think you need to complete, triage them: What can you do, delete, delegate, or defer?

Ask for help. I think of this skill as a developmental milestone for new parents. Just as your baby will learn new skills, men and women also have to learn how to be moms and dads. Asking for help when you're overwhelmed is an essential skill. Sometimes women think a "good mom" would be able to handle things on her own. I would tell you that a "good mom" is one who builds her village around her, who knows where to go for what she needs, and who gives herself grace when times are hard.

Beware the Link between Sleep Deprivation and Mood Disorders

Be alert to signs of depression and anxiety. Research is very clear: sleep deprivation can cause depression, and depression can cause disrupted sleep. If breastfeeding is going poorly, that is another risk factor for postpartum depression. If breastfeeding is going well, it is protective against depression and is correlated with improved sleep for both mother and baby.

One study found that if a mother gets four consecutive hours of sleep, her risk of depression is lower. If you can find ways to get even a four hour stretch, you may feel much better.

You already have one of life's biggest risk factors for depression and anxiety: You had a baby. Stress itself, apart from a new baby, can cause depression. Significant sleep deprivation can exacerbate any brewing mood problems, or can trigger one in a mom who was feeling okay before. Several research sources indicate that taking longer than 25 minutes to fall asleep is correlated with either a current or a developing mood disorder. The same can be said for insomnia in the middle of the night, despite having the opportunity to sleep while the rest of your family slumbers on. Be alert to your red flags.

Mild cases of postpartum depression or anxiety can be alleviated when you build in sleep, get support from a mom's group, ask for help with chores, eat well, exercise a bit, and talk to your friends. If your efforts don't make you feel better, act decisively. Prioritize yourself and call your health care team. When left untreated, postpartum depression and anxiety can be devastating to a new mother and her family.

AMMA
PARENTING CENTER

yellow light sleep

Yellow Light Sleep
When baby is 3-6 months old: Yellow means slow.
Slow down the use of sleep associations that are unsustainable.

In a Nutshell
Consistently practice sleep independence, but end the practice sessions if baby is stressed. Promote sustainable sleep associations and phase out unsustainable ones. Create daily rhythms and rituals by reinforcing emerging patterns.

Recap of the Green Light Stage Base Skills
- Create a sleep-friendly environment (page 21).
- Learn to interpret cues and cries (page 22).
- Introduce "drowsy but awake" in the third month (page 25).

The Three Base Skills You'll Learn in the Yellow Light Stage
- Work with sleep associations (page 35).
- Practice more sleep independence (page 37).
- Support emerging patterns (page 43).

Up Next in the Red Light Stage
- Nap schedules.
- Sleep teaching (also known as sleep training).

Overview of the Yellow Light Stage

With the newborn months behind him, your baby will be making sleep progress and showing more signs of maturity. Longer sleep stretches at night, deeper sleep, and emerging patterns are a welcome change. However, with the arrival of several factors that can disrupt sleep (see Sleep Sinkers, page 34), parents can be surprised by setbacks and new challenges. These months can sometimes feel extra difficult because of these ebbs and flows. This is the ideal age to start gently practicing some new skills while still giving your baby the nurturing and the connection that he needs.

Sleep at This Age

Babies will vary widely regarding many factors that affect sleep. Development, starting child care, feeding methods, temperament, and parenting styles can all play into how your baby sleeps. Some babies will show greater independence with sleep at this age, while others may still need their parents for more support. If your baby was born prematurely, you may need to set your expectations accordingly.

At this age, the average baby is spending 14-15 hours asleep per day. At 3 months many babies will nap three or more times a day, often in catnaps, and often with no particular pattern. By the 6 month, many babies are napping in three distinct naps per day.

Babies may grow into more control over their stress responses, body movement, and sleep states. The neurological arousal (I think of it as revving an engine) that a baby needs to feed or interact with her world is now more easily down regulated. This, along with the ability to maintain sleep and wakefulness called "state control," helps with sleep progress.

Babies may increasingly be able to self-soothe: entertaining themselves by looking around, playing with their hands, kicking, making noises, and engaging in other forms of fun.

Circadian rhythms mature around 12-16 weeks. This daily cycle of changes in temperature, blood pressure and hormones is important for sleep progress. Exposure to light and dark at the right times of day and night is helpful in supporting circadian rhythms. This development helps your baby consolidate sleep overnight and maintain more wakefulness during the day. By 6 months a regular bedtime and wake time help support your baby's natural circadian rhythms.

Sleep cycles are longer now, and your baby spends more time in quiet sleep. When your baby is in quiet sleep, her body will be less active and less sensitive to her environment, so she is less likely to wake up easily. Another new change is the switch to starting sleep in a quiet state and then transitioning into active sleep, which is the opposite

> **Starting in quiet sleep helps your baby learn to go down "drowsy but awake."**

of what she did as a newborn. This quiet-active order is a mature sleep pattern, and means your baby will better tolerate being put down upon becoming drowsy or after falling asleep.

Although overnight sleep is improving, many babies are still waking several times at night. At this age, babies vary widely in nighttime sleep behavior, ranging from sleeping all night to waking two or three times. Most babies at 6 months old can sleep 6 hours at a stretch at night (but may not do it every night).

Many babies are still eating several times overnight. Daytime eating patterns can affect nighttime sleep, and some breastfed babies whose mothers are working might wait for her and nurse more at night. A breastfed baby nurses for comfort and connection as well as nutrition, which may lead her to ask for you more often during the night.

> **The official definition of sleeping through the night is 5 to 6 hours in a row.**

Temperament and Sleep

As I discussed in the Green Light stage, temperament greatly affects sleep.

The personality profile of everyone in the family will affect how the family operates together, and it's helpful to understand not only your baby's temperament, but your own temperament as well.

At birth, babies do show behaviors that reflect their temperaments, but they are also exhibiting biologically driven behaviors, so discerning a temperament profile is challenging. By 4-6 months, you can see much more of their personality coming through.

Temperament can be expressed through sleep in some of these ways:

Intensity: How big are your child's reactions? How fast do you need to move when she starts showing sleepy cues?

Sensitivity: How much does the environment affect your baby? How do things like light, temperature, noise, and smells lengthen or shorten sleep?

Regularity: How consistent are your baby's eating, sleeping, and activity cycles?

Soothability: How easily can your child be calmed?

Adaptability: How flexible is your baby in regards to different sleep environments and caregivers?

For more information on temperament, visit a website called The Preventive Ounce (preventiveoz.org). For a small fee, you can complete an intake form and at the end you are given a profile of your baby's temperament. I have also included a worksheet on sleep and temperament on page 62. I think that understanding temperament is such an important part of parenting. The better you know your child and what makes him tick, the more you'll be able to make parenting decisions that best fit his needs.

Development and Sleep

When it comes to sleep, development is the engine that drives the progress. At this age, your baby's development is starting to take off, his world is expanding, and rapid changes are happening. As discussed earlier, there are many developmental changes that result in better sleep. There are also changes that can *challenge* sleep. When babies who were making progress halt or reverse that progress, I call it the "Second Quarter Slump." Understanding the causes of sleep regressions can help you navigate the setbacks and to look for tools that will help you get sleep back on track.

> The "Second Quarter Slump" is a time of sleep regressions and challenges for a baby who was previously making progress. Maintain your Base Skills and have patience.

Babies are now able to see better, so exciting sleep environments may interfere with sleep. A baby who could before sleep in the middle of errands or a social gathering may now only nap in his sleep-friendly environment. If you are working on daytime naps, then making the room even darker may help. Some parents find success with taking down interesting wall decorations, keeping exciting toys out of view, and looking for other ways to make the room boring. On several occasions, I have suggested that parents switch to white sheets when their babies were too busy trying to pick up the flowers or stripes on their sheets. One family in my sleep class found that their spirited son napped best in the walk-in closet, as it was pitch dark and extra quiet.

Interest in cause and effect can make scratching the sheets, kicking, and playing other games more fun than sleep. Screeching may result in the appearance of a parent, which is extra exciting!

The drive to practice and master fine and gross motor skills can interfere with sleep. Babies can be so driven to master a milestone that they practice at night or during naps. Many parents have been called to assist a baby who has figured out how to sit up, but not how to lie back down. The AAP recommends that babies sleep on their backs until one year of age. However, once a baby can roll comfortably from front to back and back to front, there's probably no need to roll him back onto his back if he has rolled over. If your baby doesn't like sleeping on his tummy, rest assured that he will eventually learn to stop rolling when he wants to sleep. Some babies even start sleeping better once they're on their tummies.

Fears and anxieties may begin to appear at this age. Stranger anxiety and separation anxiety can both affect sleep. If something scary or stressful happened during the day, some babies will have disrupted sleep the following night (which is true for children and adults of all ages). Emotions and worries affect sleep more at this age than they did in the newborn months.

"Sleep Sinkers"

Six disrupters, or "Sleep Sinkers," that are especially common at this age can cause sleep regressions: teething, travel, illness, developmental milestones, growth spurts, and parental stress. These are time-limited, temporary events in a baby's life, but they can have a negative impact on sleep. When your baby is coping with a Sleep Sinker, he may need extra support and comfort.

In infancy and toddlerhood, sleep disturbances can seem never ending, like they happen one after the other. Precious progress can be reversed as babies rotate constantly from one Sleep Sinker to the next. (See the "Second Quarter Slump," page 33).

> **When in a "Sleep Sinker," have patience and keep up your Base Skills.**

I like to tell parents, "Inconsistency is your new consistency." If there's one thing you can rely on, it's that everything at this age is a phase, even the good things. As babies approach the Red Light stage and their first birthday, these big ups and downs usually settle down a bit.

During sleep regressions, be flexible and respond attentively to your baby when he needs you. Keep up with your Base Skills to prevent sleep from becoming completely unraveled when coping with sleep regressions. If you are working with your baby on new sleep skills, wait until the Sleep Sinkers have passed or are winding down before you ask your baby to practice independence.

The First Yellow Light Base Skill: Working with Sleep Associations

Triggers for, or associations with, sleep can be easy to maintain, like a dark room and white noise. Or they can require an effort on your part, like nursing, holding, swinging, rocking, or bouncing. Now is a good time to start being thoughtful about which associations you want your child to have: Introduce sustainable associations, and tease out ones that have become unsustainable.

If something makes you both happy, and you are willing to keep it up, then there's no need to change. Sometimes parents are afraid of creating bad habits, or feel pressure from friends and family to stop something that is enjoyable and that works for their family. If you treasure those moments rocking your baby to sleep at bedtime, and it's not causing disruptions in your baby's sleep, by all means keep going. Babies and parents alike need those sweet, snuggly moments with each other. Working parents especially treasure the connection time. Breastfeeding mothers and babies use nursing to connect, comfort, and sustain each other, and nursing a sleepy baby down to sleep in a quiet, dark nursery can be some of the sweetest moments of motherhood.

Some babies become reliant on a parent's actions for sleep so much that they cannot get back to sleep from a "Fake Wake" (see page 16) in the night without it. If that loving rocking has now become such a strong association that your baby needs to be rocked to sleep many times a night, and your baby is now becoming sleep deprived because of the chronic disruption, then you can gently withdraw it and replace it with other associations. With the next Base Skill, "Practicing sleep independence," we'll explore how to phase out an unsustainable sleep association and encourage more independence.

Before withdrawing a sleep association, first establish positive and sustainable associations that your baby can use as alternatives. Once you've given your baby plenty of support, you can start withdrawing unsustainable sleep associations.

In the Green Light stage, you learned about the Base Skill of creating a sleep-friendly environment (page 21); those tactics not only promote good sleep, but they also serve as environmental sleep associations. If you have been using a dark room and white noise machine for sleep, you have already been using wonderful sleep associations. Here are more examples of age-appropriate, sustainable sleep associations.

Transitional objects. A small mini-blanket, or "lovey," can be a wonderful baby-led sleep association. Select a small, handkerchief-sized lovey made of light, breathable fabric (put it over your own mouth to test whether your baby can breathe through it). I strongly recommend buying two identical lovies and using them in regular rotation so that they each get the same wear. If one ever gets lost, your baby may reject the backup if it doesn't have the same familiar texture and smell.

Start introducing the lovey by simply including it in the bedtime routine (see below). Snuggle with the lovey as you nurse or bottle feed, sing songs, read stories, and do other calming rituals. Over time, your baby will associate the lovey with sleep, and it will become a sleep cue. He'll also associate it with you and your reassuring presence. By 6-12 months, most pediatricians give the okay to leave the lovey in the crib with your baby. If your baby is not old enough, or your pediatrician says "not yet," then keep it as a part of the bedtime routine, but do not give it to your child for sleep. Once you are given permission to leave the lovey in the crib, consider keeping it as a sleep-only association. If it becomes a toy and is used in play or when your baby is out of his sleep environment, then it may not be as strong a sleep trigger. Some families have an "only-in-the-crib" rule (of course, this includes the crib at child care).

Aromatherapy. A dab of lavender balm or other essential oil can be an additional sleep cue. Scent is a powerful memory trigger, and if you include a calming scent during each evening's bedtime routine, it can be a wonderful sleep association. Some parents love it so much that they start dabbing it on their own pillows!

A bedtime routine. A short, calming routine right before bed has been shown many times in research to help babies sleep. When considering a bedtime routine for your family, here are some guidelines.

> The bedtime routine should be completed by the time sleepy cues start (page 22). This means you need to start the routine about 15 to 30 minutes *before you anticipate sleep cues*. At first, this can be a moving target, but try your best. After a while, the routine itself will cue your baby that it's time to sleep.
>
> Keep the routine short and simple. Lowering the lights, turning on

the white noise, using a calm voice, aromatherapy, and snuggling with the lovey can accompany stories and songs. Each component should be easy and brief enough that a babysitter could do it, or that you could speed it up a bit if you're running behind or if your baby is extra tired. The ideal bedtime routine lasts anywhere from 15 to 30 minutes.

If you are working on separating feeding from sleep (as described in the next Base Skill), then you could put feeding first in the lineup, followed by the rest of the routine. Your baby should lie down drowsy but awake.

Different caregivers will have different styles, and there are many right ways to put a baby to bed. As long as the basics are consistent, it's fine to have mildly different variations of the bedtime routine.

Pacifiers and swaddlers can start out as sleep aids, but sometimes can progress into sleep disrupters at this age. If they are working well, then there's no need to phase them out too soon. If they are starting to interfere with sleep, then keep reading to learn how to phase them out.

The Second Yellow Light Base Skill: Practicing Independence

At this age, your baby may be developmentally ready to practice more sleep independence and self-soothing. If you haven't started "drowsy but awake," now is a good time. To nudge your baby to sleep more independently, you can, if you choose, now offer opportunities to practice what I call **the "Big Three" skills**:

- Lying down for sleep drowsy but awake,
- on a flat motionless surface,
- while not actively eating.

These three skills are helpful for long-term sleep quality because dependence on being held, being in motion, and eating down into sleep can be habits that disrupt sleep as time goes on. In these next sections, I'll teach you ways to gently introduce some independence through practice sessions.

Remember, babies and parents need to come to readiness in their own time. Babies often need their parents' support for sleep well throughout their first year. It's up to you to decide the sleep culture in your family. You get to choose when and whether to phase out holding, feeding, and motion. Some high-needs babies with spirited temperaments arrive at sleep independence much later than other babies, and <u>need</u> parent-led sleep support. Do what works for your baby and your family.

About Practice Sessions

"Practice sessions" are short periods of time spent doing something that you consider to be a new sleep skill. Your baby may fuss or cry briefly while practicing. Dissatisfaction or frustration often accompanies learning (the same goes for learning how to roll over and other milestones).

If dissatisfaction turns to *distress*, and your baby's cry tells you that he's done practicing, then take a break or stop the practice session. Once babies are distressed, crying too hard, or overtired, they are no longer learning. If, after settling your baby, you think that he could try again, then you can try some more practicing. If you sense that your baby is getting overtired or is just emotionally done, stop and go back to what works. Practice the new skill again another time.

> When your baby goes from dissatisfaction to distress, she is no longer learning. Stop and try again at the next sleep episode. The AAP recommends no more than 10 minutes of crying without comfort when working with sleep.

What do I mean when I draw a line between dissatisfaction and distress? The answer is in the quality of the cry. (Here's where your auditory cue reading skills come in handy; see page 22.) When a baby is learning something that pushes his comfort level, he may fuss, grunt, groan, and squawk. You know those noises well, probably from tummy time, or from back in the newborn weeks during The Fussies (see page 17). I'm talking about the moment when those "I'm keeping it together" sounds give way to "I don't have it together anymore" sounds: outright crying in a way that tells you that he needs you. When you hear that cry, trust your caring instincts and go to him. The American Academy of Pediatrics recommends that you do not let your baby cry for more than 10 minutes without being comforted when working with sleep.

Depending on your baby's temperament, those learning moments can last minutes or just seconds. Some babies go from dissatisfied to distressed very fast! Spirited babies, if pushed past a certain emotional comfort point, may really lose it and have a hard time recovering, and you don't want to hit that point.

Remember that however long your baby spent practicing, whether it was five seconds or five minutes, he was learning.

When teaching new skills, set your baby up for success. Read cues and cries correctly, use a sleep-friendly environment, and offer plenty of sustainable environmental and baby-led sleep associations. Give him the best possible chance at mastering a new skill.

Practice at Your Baby's Pace

The process of learning to sleep independently varies widely for children. Some babies pick up these new skills quickly and are adaptable and flexible. Other children will take their time getting used to a new level of independence from their parents. A baby has to have a certain level of neurologic maturity to modulate their stress responses. Have respect for your child's emotional needs, developmental readiness, and tolerance for stress when teaching new sleep skills. If it's not working, then wait a while and try again later. Remember, your baby is very young right now, and needs security and trust.

Sleep independence can be more of a stretch for children with "spirited" temperaments. These are children who are more intense, more sensitive, less adaptable, or less soothable than others (or maybe all of the above). Spirited infants need more sleep support from their caregivers, and learning new skills can take longer and may not be successful until they have had more time to mature. If you have a spirited infant, understand that your baby may need more support and more time.

Learning a new skill is sometimes best done in stages. If your baby is used to nursing down to sleep and napping in your arms, then you may want to teach him how to fall asleep without nursing first, and once he's mastered that teach him how to sleep out of your arms.

Babies with acid reflux disease may not tolerate lying flat until the reflux has completely resolved. Focus on other skills until he outgrows the reflux.

If your baby was born prematurely, then he may be a bit behind in his sleep abilities. When it comes to sleep, I recommend thinking of your baby's age as from the due date rather than the birth date.

Practice these skills only when your baby is not in a Sleep Sinker, when he is in a good mood, and when *you* are ready. If you are experiencing stress or a life transition of your own, you may not be emotionally available enough to teach patiently. Wait until you are in a place of readiness as a teacher. In the meantime, keep up with the other Base Skills: cue reading, providing a sleep-friendly environment, and creating sustainable sleep associations.

Don't Push It

It's easy to get discouraged and to think that you are "caving in" if you end a practice session and go back to what works. Be assured that even a few moments of practicing was a learning moment for your baby. Ending the practice session isn't failing, it's responding appropriately to your baby's needs. You can be confident responding this way, because you know that there are many sleep opportunities in the day and that your baby can practice again next time.

> Don't sacrifice sleep for learning. In other words, if your baby becomes overtired from all the practicing, then it's not worth it! Sleep is more important than independence right now. You may have more success in a few weeks, or if you go at a slower pace.

Remember, it's important for your baby to get good sleep. Although you may want to hurry learning along, if your baby is becoming overtired with all the effort of practicing, then you might be moving too fast. Maybe all he can do is one or two practice sessions a day. Babies don't learn well when they're overtired, so don't sacrifice sleep for learning.

Let's Look at Some Examples of Practice Sessions

1. Your baby usually naps in your arms, and you want to teach her to sleep in her crib. When you see her getting drowsy, put her in her crib (which you've put in a sleep-friendly environment). Wait and watch. She may fuss a little because she is out of your arms, but give her a few moments of trying. If her cries escalate, then put your hands on her body, lean in close (you may need a step stool by the crib) and shush and rock her gently without picking her up. See if she can fall asleep with this extra support. If she continues to escalate and she becomes distressed, then stop the practice session, pick her up, and give her the support she needs to take a good nap. Practice *again* at the next sleep opportunity.

2. You are teaching your baby to separate feeding from sleeping. When you see the signs of drowsiness at the breast or bottle, take your baby off and see if he will fall asleep without eating. Wait and watch. If he escalates, then start rocking, shushing, or giving other support. If he continues to escalate and becomes distressed, then return him to the bottle or the breast until he falls asleep. Practice *again* at the next sleep opportunity.

3. You are teaching your baby to sleep on a flat, motionless surface when she's used to sleeping in a moving swing. Move the swing into the sleep-friendly environment. When your baby shows drowsy cues but is still conscious, put her in the swing but put it on a lower motion setting than usual. Wait and watch. If she starts escalating, then quicken the swing until she calms, but slow it down again when she starts to fall asleep. If she can tolerate another practice session, then keep repeating this until she falls asleep in the slower setting. If she escalates and is truly done with practice, then give her what she needs to have a successful nap and try again at the next sleep opportunity. When she is used to swinging at a slower speed, start practicing an even lower speed or motionless. Then you can try the crib.

About Pacifiers

Babies who rely on pacifiers for soothing may wake and get frustrated if the pacifier falls out in the night. With increasing dependence on the pacifier, sleep may become disrupted over time, and a sleep helper can turn into a Sleep Sinker. If pacifiers are hindering rather than helping, you have a few options. You can wait it out until your baby develops the ability to replace his own pacifier, which may be several months from now. In the meantime, you can replace it for him overnight when he cries. Use a pacifier with a small plush toy sewn on (a "Wub-a-Nub") so that he can grasp it more easily as he learns to do it himself.

Or you can phase out the pacifier. This can be done gradually by using the techniques described in the Base Skill "Practicing More Sleep Independence" (see page 37). Perhaps you practice falling asleep without a pacifier during the night first, and then later during the day (be sure to offer other soothing). Or you can phase both days and nights out at the same time. Your plan will depend on how opinionated your baby is, and how reluctantly he responds to transitions.

Another option is to go "cold turkey" and do away with them altogether at once. Make sure you're providing other soothing to your baby, and expect a few rough days and nights while he learns. Rest assured that your baby will learn how to sleep without a pacifier just fine. Have confidence in his abilities!

About Swaddling

Swaddling with arms wrapped in should be discontinued before your baby starts rolling from back to front, or when swaddling becomes disruptive to sleep (the AAP recommends stopping swaddling at 2 months to avoid the possibility of rolling in a swaddle). Some babies at this age are eager to have more mobility at night, and not having access to arms and hands may frustrate them. How you discontinue the swaddle will depend on why you are doing it.

> **Swaddling with arms wrapped in should be discontinued before your baby learns to roll.**

If your baby has rolled onto his stomach with his arms inaccessible, the swaddle needs to be discontinued right away for safety reasons. This abrupt stop will result in a few rough days and nights, but your baby must be able to protect his airway while lying on his stomach, and he needs his arms to push his upper body up. If you must stop cold turkey, then give your baby lots of additional support and expect a few rough days and nights. Baby Merlin's Magic Sleep Suit is a padded suit that muffles the baby's twitches, yet leaves hands and arms free. Our clients love this product as a step-down from swaddling. You can also just wrap the swaddling product around your baby's chest, which gives reassuring pressure and leaves the arms free. Be sure that the swaddling product cannot become a suffocation hazard.

If you have more time to phase out the swaddle slowly, try a "half wrap": either swaddle with one arm out, or with both hands up by his face and the wrap across his forearms. Once he is used to this, move to both arms free and a wrap across his chest (many babies like a little pressure on their chests). You can then move to just pajamas or a sleep sack. Baby Merlin's Magic Sleep Suit is a good option for this situation as well.

The Third Yellow Light Base Skill: Support Emerging Patterns

At three to six months, babies may thrive on predictable daily rhythms and routines. As you see more patterns emerge, like falling asleep at the same time for a nap or at night, reinforce those emerging patterns by offering sleep at the anticipated sleepy time.

There are three key sleep episodes during the day: the morning nap, the naplet, and bedtime.

Naps

The naps at the beginning and end of the day are the most important. What happens during the rest of the day isn't as crucial and can vary widely. Many babies are cat napping throughout the middle of the day, with nap length ranging from 40 to 90 minutes. As they approach 6 months, you may see the emergence of a three-nap pattern. For now, it's enough to protect the two "bookend" naps.

The Morning Nap

The onset of the morning nap is often within 45 to 90 minutes of waking up. When your baby wakes up for the day, open the curtains and spend some time in full-spectrum morning light (or if the weather is nice, then you could spend a few minutes outside). Watch for nap readiness soon after this brief wakeful period. Some babies don't even have time to get out of their pajamas!

A good morning nap sets the tone for the rest of the day's sleep, so protect it: put your baby in a sleep-friendly environment and try not to wake your baby. If your baby becomes overtired this early in the day, sleep may be difficult for the rest of the day and overnight as the overtired hormones accumulate.

For working parents, the morning nap might be in the car on the way to childcare, or right after drop off. For at-home parents, this would be a good nap to take in the crib because your baby often sleeps deeply and is able to be a bit more independent than during the lighter, shorter midday naps.

The Naplet

Many babies take a 30 to 45 minute catnap late in the afternoon. This is another important sleep episode. Again, babies in childcare may take this nap in the car on the way home.

Anticipate sleepy cues for bedtime within 60-120 minutes of awaking from the naplet. For busy families, this can be a hard time of day. Remember that the bedtime routine should start early enough so that your baby is in the crib with lights out when the sleepy cues start. This may mean that you only have 30 to 60 minutes of time between the end of the naplet and the start of the bedtime routine.

Bedtime

Now is a good age to ensure that your baby is going to bed at the *just-right* time. Getting to sleep at the natural bedtime will improve your baby's overnight sleep and will set him up for good sleep the next day. Watch for sleep cues carefully, and remember that at this age, your baby's bedtime may move earlier and earlier. A common bedtime range for this age group is 6 to 8 pm.

Ideally, the bedtime routine will be completed by the time your baby starts showing drowsy cues. This may mean starting the bedtime

> **A bedtime routine at the just-right time of night is one of the most important things you can do to promote good sleep. Cues, not clocks, determine the just-right time.**

routine when your baby is showing no signs of sleepiness! Be assured that over time, the routine itself will become a wonderful sleep association and will cue your baby for sleep.

Some parents worry that an early bedtime may mean that their baby wakes more times at night to eat than she did with a late bedtime. If the night now encompasses twelve hours, this may in fact be the case, but it is still important to follow the natural bedtime. You may try adding a dream feed (see below).

Night Sleep

Most babies at 6 months are sleeping in stretches of six hours or more (this is the medical definition of sleeping through the night). That still leaves some babies who cannot yet sleep 6 consecutive hours in a row – never fear! This too shall pass. It's very common for 3- to 6-month-old babies to still be eating or waking a few times at night. Young babies often still need nurturing at night, and some night waking is normal at this age. Most babies will eat or have a short snuggle and then go right back to sleep. Breastfed babies nurse for both food and connection. It is normal for them to nurse a few times at night at this age. If your breastfed baby is in daycare, then this might be especially true. Many mothers keep night nursing in order to maintain an abundant milk supply, especially if they are working.

If your baby wakes repeatedly, is overly agitated, or can't fall back asleep easily, then you may want to look into causes. Is your baby in a Sleep Sinker (see page 35)? Is he overtired? Look for signs of being overtired during the day, as this can disrupt sleep even into the night. Sometimes a quick fix, like moving the bedtime earlier, later, or offering more naps, can help with overnight sleep.

Phasing Down Overnight Eating

As a lactation consultant, my preference is to let babies be in charge of when to stop eating overnight (within reason, of course). I see most babies spontaneously stop eating at night somewhere between 5 and 9 months, with a few holding on until their first birthday. If you are feeding your baby many times at night or are reaching your breaking point and want to see if he's ready to drop a feeding, then here are some strategies:

<u>Try to front-load calories during the day by offering more feedings.</u> Starting baby food early has not been proven to improve overnight sleep. Offer more milk or formula, which is richer in protein and fat than baby food is.

Babies in daycare may be too distracted to eat much, and may "reverse cycle," or wait for a quiet, calm house at night in which to eat. Breastfeeding moms and babies may appreciate the snuggle time and the boost in milk supply. Reverse cycling is not necessarily a problem unless you are becoming exhausted and want to make a change, in which case you could work with your baby's caregiver on strategies to promote better eating at daycare. Promoting better intake during the day and phasing down overnight eating at night will usually do the trick. (Be alert to a lower milk supply: you may still need to pump at night.)

<u>Try a "dream feed."</u> At about 10 pm, quietly go to your baby and offer a meal. Stimulate your baby as little as possible: no talking, playing, diaper changing, or light. Your baby may "sleep-eat" and take in enough calories to last a few hours so you can get a stretch of good sleep. Be forewarned that dream feeds may not be effective, or may make sleep even worse.

<u>Try the "feed last" approach.</u> When your baby wakes up, and you are suspicious that he may not be truly hungry, try other soothing strategies before feeding. Feed as a last resort. You may target certain wakings and not others for this approach. If your baby just slept for 4 to 6 hours and you are relatively certain that he's truly hungry, then just feed him. "Feed last" is a good approach for the wakings that you think may not be caused by true hunger. Of course, if you have tried other comforting but your baby persists, then trust that he is genuinely hungry. He is still young and overnight eating is normal.

<u>Try phasing out a particular feeding.</u> Target a feeding you want to eliminate, and slowly taper down the minutes at the breast or ounces in the bottle at that time. Finish the feeding right at the moment that you think she is satisfied enough but not quite finished. Over the course of a week or two, see if you can get all the way down to 2 ounces in the bottle or 2 minutes at the breast. When you get down to 2 minutes or 2 ounces you can stop that feed completely. Be respectful if your baby resists and is not yet ready to drop that feed. You can always wait a few weeks and try again later.

AMMA
PARENTING CENTER

red light sleep

When baby is 6-12 months old: Red means woah! Put the brakes on unsustainable sleep associations now. They may be more challenging to stop as baby gets older.

In a Nutshell

Nap schedules and sleep consolidation emerge at this age. If you need to make changes, then you can start sleep interventions with love and consistency, taking temperament into account. Keep your Base Skills going when troubleshooting sleep regressions.

Recap of the Green Light Stage and Yellow Light Stage Base Skills
- Create a sleep-friendly environment (page 21).
- Interpret cues and cries (page 22).
- Introduce "drowsy but awake" in the third month (page 25).
- Work with sleep associations (page 35).
- Practice more sleep independence (page 37).
- Support emerging patterns (page 43).

Overview of the Red Light Stage

Your baby is at least halfway to his first birthday! New developmental milestones seem to pop up all of the time, and your baby is changing so fast. If you have been working on sleep in the Yellow Light stage, then your efforts may start to pay off now. Many babies can now fall asleep without much help, stay asleep for most of the night, and use self-soothing strategies like tummy sleeping, loveys, thumb sucking, listening to white noise, etc. In the Red Light stage, I'll focus on nap schedules and as-needed sleep interventions.

Sleep at This Age

In the second half of the year, your baby's circadian rhythms are more developed, and their bodies respond well to a schedule. They build up the drive to sleep (called sleep pressure) during the day and that sustains long sleep stretches at night.

> If your older baby is fighting sleep at bedtime, or talking in her crib for a long while, then you may need to push the bedtime back so that she's good and sleepy. Being "under tired" can create problems for night sleep.

Regular bedtimes and wake times support the natural cyclical patterns of circadian rhythm.

At 6-9 months, babies average about 13-16 hours of sleep per day, 10-12 of which is at night. One or two feedings overnight is not unusual, nor is nursing for comfort and connection, although some babies no longer eat at night by about 9 months. Most babies at 6 months old will sleep at least six uninterrupted hours, but they may not do it every night. Sleeping 5-6 hours in a row is the medical definition of "sleeping through the night."

By 9 months, you may start to see a two-nap pattern emerge as baby drops the late afternoon nap and consolidates daytime sleep. Total daytime sleep averages 3 to 4 hours during this time. Your baby may consolidate these two naps into one main nap between 12 and 18 months. Dropping naps usually brings about some temporary challenges as your baby gets used to her new normal.

Your baby may now stay awake for 2 to 4 hours at a stretch. The days of offering frequent sleep like you did in the newborns months are over. Your baby may need to be adequately tired now in order to fall asleep well. Luckily, with milestones like crawling, pulling up, and stepping, all that daily activity can help tucker her out.

Fears and Anxieties

Babies at this age can be prone to fears and anxieties. Stranger anxiety and separation anxiety can both interrupt sleep. Parents sometimes report hearing true fear or even terror in their baby's cries. Babies who once slept peacefully in a very dark room may now become fearful, and may benefit from a small red night light. Babies who were sleeping through the night may awaken and need reassurance from you. If your baby's day was particularly stimulating, or she was exposed to something scary or new, sleep may be disrupted. Have patience and know that these fears are developmentally normal and will resolve in time. Hold steady to your Base Skills and allow for extra snuggles and reassurance when needed. If your baby needs increasingly frequent parenting at night and you suspect that your nocturnal comfort is turning into a habit or sleep association, then slowly phase it out using the "Practicing Independence" strategies discussed in the Yellow Light (page 37).

Schedules

Because babies often thrive when regular wake-ups, naps and bedtimes are built into daily rhythms, 6 to 12 months is a good time to nudge your baby onto a schedule if she isn't on one already. Two naps a day is the most common pattern by 9 to 12 months. The length of the naps may vary, but the average total daytime sleep is 3 to 4 hours.

> **Both overtired and undertired can negatively affect night sleep. When troubleshooting, try to make sure the amount of daytime sleep, the bedtime and the wake-up are all just-right for your baby.**

Babies often spend increasingly longer stretches awake as the day goes on. The morning nap may only be 90-120 minutes after waking up from the night, whereas there may be up to 4 hours between the afternoon nap and bedtime (provided there is no naplet). At this age, your baby may not fall asleep if she's not sleepy enough, so enough awake time becomes important. Oversleeping (sleeping in too long, or naps that are too long) can negatively affect your baby's ability to fall asleep at the next sleep episode. Giving your baby lots of floor play, playtime with other babies, and time outside can help get her nice and tired for the next nap.

Most babies have phased out the brief "naplet" in the late afternoon by 9 months. When the naplet disappears, it gets absorbed into night sleep, making bedtime shift a bit earlier. When your baby is in the process of dropping the naplet, he may fight sleep at the usual time, simultaneously refusing to go to sleep and getting more tired as the day goes on. You can support and distract him as best you can and temporarily move bedtime earlier to meet his sleep needs. It can take a few weeks of adjustment when your baby is dropping a nap.

To nudge your baby onto a daily schedule, keep the morning wake-up and bedtime consistent to support your baby's circadian rhythm. In the early months our mantra was "cues not clocks", and now we say "cues and clocks". During the day aim for consistent nap times, and cue sleep with some simple mini-routines and sleep associations like white noise, a dark room, a sleep sack, a lovey, etc. End each nap with turning on the lights, turning off the white noise machine, a cheerful "good morning!" and some quiet play to transition your baby to wakefulness.

On your journey towards a daytime schedule you may need to occasionally wake your baby from one sleep episode to protect the next nap or bedtime. Wake her slowly and gently when you see she is in a light sleep state by gradually increasing the light in the room, turning off the white noise, making some sounds, and patting her back. Be aware that shortchanging naps can lead to overtired and sleep deficits, so be watchful. If your baby tends to be a big napper and still has great overnight sleep, than don't fix it because

> **Naps are tricky, plain and simple. Sometimes, there's no easy path to a clean and tidy nap schedule. Do your best.**

it's not broken. If overnight sleep is poor because your baby is sleeping too much in the day, slowly pare back daytime sleep gradually, not reducing naps by more than 15 to 20 minutes at a time.

Naps are tricky. Try not to get discouraged if your baby doesn't sleep consistently, long enough, or on a schedule. Daytime sleep can take a long time to mature, and some kids are just never going to be great nappers. Aim for making things better, not perfect.

Correcting Unwanted Sleep Behaviors

Up to 45% of parents report a sleep problem in the second 6 months of life. Research shows that babies with sleep problems may not outgrow them with time; rather they can persist into toddlerhood and beyond without the proper intervention.

What's important here is how you define a "sleep problem." Sometimes, parents identify something as a problem or crutch when I would call it a strategy! I have had many experiences in classes when a family realizes that the "problem," whether it's bed sharing, nursing to sleep, holding for naps or feeding at night, is only a problem to other people. If it's working

If it's not broken, then don't fix it.

in your family and everyone is safely getting enough sleep, then it's not a problem, and it doesn't need to be fixed.

On the other hand, if you or your baby are becoming sleep deprived because she has a sleep association that cannot be sustained, or because she is waking so many times at night that you or she cannot function during the day, or because she is so overtired that she can't get good sleep... then that's a problem.

Significant and chronic sleep deprivation can affect a child's cognitive development, mood regulation, attention and behavior, and health. Sleep deprivation in mothers has been correlated with depression and can negatively affect family functioning. I want to reassure you that if you or your baby are suffering it is *okay* to make a change. You *can* safely and effectively make sleep better while following your caring instincts.

Research also shows that many different sleep-teaching techniques are effective: one large meta-analysis of 52 sleep training studies showed that 82% of babies will respond to sleep interventions with improved sleep (Mindell et al, 2006). Another study followed 225 children over 5 years to determine benefits and harms of sleep training. When done by gradual sleep training methods like "controlled crying" (*Solving Your Child's Sleep Problems* by Richard Ferber or *The SleepEasy Solution* by Jennifer Waldburger and Jill Spivack) or "camping out" (*The Sleep Lady's Good Night, Sleep Tight* by Kim West) there were no demonstrated negative effects on emotional development, emotional health, or the parent-child bond (Price et al, 2012). Interestingly, no long-term benefits were observed, either.

Many books give parents the okay to sleep train starting at 4 months. Why does our Sleep Stoplight® wait until 6-12 months? First, it's my hope that all the gentle practicing that you did from months 3 to 6 has left you with a baby who doesn't need a dramatic intervention. The whole purpose of my system is to avoid cry-based sleep training. If you have a 6-12 month-old and are considering sleep training, but haven't tried the Base Skills from the Green and Yellow Lights, then spend a few weeks implementing them. You may be surprised at the progress your baby can make with just those strategies alone. Second, research on the neurologic ability of babies to regulate their behavioral responses and calm themselves (a result of the myelenation of the vagus nerve) indicates that this physical process is occurring at a rapid rate up through approximately 6 months (and doesn't complete until adolescence). A thorough discussion of the science behind the vagus nerve and its development can be found in the article by Stephen Porgess and Senta Furman (2011) listed in the Bibliography. Although some babies will fare well with sleep interventions before 6 months, we would like to set babies up for success by ensuring that their nervous systems are developmentally ready to handle stress. Ultimately, you know best how and when to ask your baby to learn new skills.

Sleep Interventions Done the Amma Way

The Green Light and Yellow Light have been all about learning your baby, supporting his development, and gently nudging him to learn new skills while staying connected and being respectful of his abilities. It will come as no surprise that when it comes to sleep interventions, I advise

> I define "cry-it-out" as sleep training systems that push your baby past the point of stress.

you to not suddenly switch to a cry-it-out system. I define "cry-it-out" systems as those that push the baby past the point of stress. Your baby is still young and still needs to trust you and to stay connected. *And there are other ways to accomplish your goals.* You can make plenty of sleep progress and successfully correct most unwanted sleep habits by gentler methods. My advice for sleep interventions in the Red Light is the same as it's been all along: understand your baby's cues, give him a successful environment, support him with lots of sustainable sleep associations and with the right daily rhythms, and then gently tease out unwanted sleep behaviors. If done at your baby's pace, then there won't be too much crying.

When working on sleep independence in the Red Light, use the same practice sessions we talked about in the Yellow Light (page 37). At each practice session, let your baby learn, even if frustrated or crying a little, until he reaches the tipping point. You will know the point of distress by the way that the cry sounds. Some babies can practice a new skill for quite a while before they hit their limit; others can only practice for a few moments. When ending a practice session, even if it was just a few minutes

> **Use distress cues, not clocks, if following sleep training systems. Let your baby cry for no more than 10 minutes at a time.**

or moments, rest assured that any small steps towards your goal count as progress. This slower, more responsive approach will take longer, but it creates less stress and supports your caring instincts. Rest assured that over time your baby *will* become more independent.

There are lots of sleep training books and systems on the market. Should you choose to consider a more assertive approach, I would urge you to implement it with the goal of progress without distress. Even the American Academy of Pediatrics recommends letting a baby cry for no longer than 10 minutes at a time when sleep training. Some authors will promise results in just a few days, or urge you to push crying too far. For methods that use a clock to time out a certain length of crying, ask yourself, "Does this work for my baby? How does this feel to me?" Check in with your own emotions and be sure that you are not sleep training a baby too quickly out of your own desperation.

What's Wrong with Crying?

It depends. We all know that babies cry for many reasons. Crying is what gets their needs met, reflects emotions, and blows off steam. When parents are connected and responsive, there is no harm in some crying. I become concerned when very young babies are pushed into sleep independence too young, too fast, or too harshly. This happens more often when parents are emotionally depleted, sleep deprived, and have hit their own breaking point. When working on sleep independence out of desperation, you may be more likely to push sleep interventions too fast. Your family can become stressed and disconnected. You may be less sensitive to your baby's cues and less sympathetic. And your baby, who has learned nothing but love and support from you thus far, is suddenly asked to reverse her expectations and understand independence in a few short days. If you need to do a sleep intervention, then approach it when you are not on the verge of desperation and have the patience to plan it out and devote the necessary time.

When Sleep Training Is Too Hard

Some babies have genuine medical reasons for disrupted sleep. Chronic ear infections, gastroesophageal reflux disease, sleep apnea, and hyperthyroid are all examples of conditions that may interfere with sleep. Contact your baby's doctor if your efforts are not met with any progress or sleep becomes worse.

About 15% of babies have a "spirited" or high-needs temperament. These babies require an individualized approach that uses the unique strategies and skills needed to parent them. These babies may have a lower tolerance for stress, and their neurologic systems may not yet be capable of self-soothing. *Raising Your Spirited Child* by Mary Sheedy Kurcinka is a valuable resource. In general, I have found these babies to fare much better when their families are very patient and gradual with their approaches and don't set their expectations too high. Time invested in a nurtured, connected babyhood will help these spirited babies grow into secure and trusting children and adults who have a lot to offer the world!

Self Care When Sleep is Hard

We've previously discussed how to tend to your own needs when parenting a young infant (page 26). As your baby grows, you still need to nurture yourself as a parent. If you are working on sleep interventions or waiting patiently until your baby outgrows a tough sleep phase, be sure to build in your own rest where you can. Go to bed early, take turns overnight with a partner, and build in restoration during the day where possible. Perhaps exercise helps you manage stress, or a long soak in a bubble bath. Tending to your own physical and emotional needs helps you be a more patient mom or dad, which in turn helps you slow down to your baby's pace.

Other Sleep Intervention Tips

When working on sleep improvement, I recommend you keep a sleep log. Sleep logs help you see patterns and chart successes. There are many sites online that have sleep logs that you may download for free.

It is often easier to work on nights first, when your baby is most tired and least likely to resist a new skill. Once you have some success with the changes that you are making at night, you can apply them to daytime sleep.

Consistency is important, and babies learn best when they know what to expect. Try to have everyone on your baby's care team on the same plan.

Have faith. Don't give up on your little learner. If your sleep improvement tactics are met with resistance, back off and try again in a few weeks, or try a slower approach.

Remember: Teaching new sleep skills with love and patience can benefit everyone. There are many right ways to approach sleep: *You* get to choose what works for your baby and for your family.

In Conclusion

I hope you have taken away many pearls of wisdom from this book. Even more than the tips and tricks, I hope you have also gotten a sense of my confidence in you as a parent: confidence that you will learn about your baby, trust your instincts, and find your own path. Sleep challenges can be some of the first parenting hurdles we face as new moms and dads. With some education, a positive attitude, patience, and a lot of love, you can teach your baby positive sleep skills.

Night-night,

Sara

Acknowledgements

This little book was "born" with the help of several midwives. Thanks to the contributions and wisdom of the teachers at Amma Parenting Center, who are in the trenches every day helping families with sleep. Thank you to Laurel Wills and Mary Sheedy Kurcinka, whose depth of expertise contributed greatly, and with whom I share an abiding love of science. Thank you to Meg Casano, Erin Evans, and Nancy Holtzman for generously sharing their knowledge with us all. Thanks to Melissa Helland who came up with the idea of a stoplight for teaching. Thank you for the editing prowess of Clare Ceballos, Melissa Sperl Thompson, Mercedes Sheldon and Shannon Keogue. And the biggest thanks goes to the parents and babies who have let me share in their journeys over the years.

Bibliography

"Blue Light Has a Dark Side." Harvard Health Letter. Harvard Medical School. May 2012.
  Web. Accessed 30 Dec. 2013.

Blyton, D.M., C.E. Sullivan, and N. Edwards. "Lactation Is Associated with an Increase in
  Slow-Wave Sleep in Women." *Journal of Sleep Research.* 11.4 (2002): 297-303.

Burnham, Melissa M., Beth L. Goodlin-Jones, Erika E. Gaylor, and Thomas F. Anders.
  "Nighttime Sleep-Wake Patterns and Self-Soothing from Birth to One Year
  of Age: A Longitudinal Intervention Study." *Journal of Child Psychology and
  Psychiatry* 43.6 (2002): 713-725.

Coons, S., and C. Guilleminault. "Development of Sleep-Wake Patterns and Non-rapid
  Eye Movement Sleep Stages during the First Six Months of Life in Normal Infants."
  Pediatrics 69.6 (1982): 793-798.

Diamond, Jared. *The World Until Yesterday: What Can We Learn from Traditional
  Societies?* New York: Penguin, 2013.

Ferber, Richard. *Solve Your Child's Sleep Problems: New, Revised, and Expanded Edition.*
  New York: Simon and Schuster, 2006.

Goyal, D., C. Gay, K. Lee. "Fragmented maternal sleep is more strongly correlated with
  depressive symptoms than infant temperament at three months." *Archives of
  Women's Mental Health* 12.4 (2009): 229-237.

Jenni, Oska G., and Bonnie B. O'Connor. "Children's Sleep: An Interplay Between Culture
  and Biology." *Pediatrics* 115.1 (2005): 204-215.

Karp, Harvey. *The Happiest Baby Guide to Great Sleep.* New York: Harper Collins, 2012.

Kendall-Tackett, Kathleen, Zhen Cong, Thomas Hale. (2011). "The Effect of Feeding
  Method on Sleep Duration, Maternal Well-Being, and Postpartum Depression."
  Clinical Lactation 2.2 (2011): 22-26.

Kurcinka, Mary Sheedy. *Raising Your Spirited Child.* New York: William Morrow, 2006.

Mannel, Rebecca, Patricia J. Martins, and Marsha Walker, eds. *Core Curriculum for
  Lactation Consultant Practice.* 3rd ed. Burlington: Jones and Bartlett Learning,
  Mass., 2012.

McGraw, Kate, Robert Hoffmann, Chris Harker, and John H. Herman. "The Development
  of Circadian Rhythms in a Human Infant." *Sleep* 22.3 (1999): 303-310.

Middlemiss, Wendy, and Kathleen Kendall-Tackett, eds. *The Science of Mother-Infant
  Sleep: Current Findings on Bedsharing, Breastfeeding, Sleep Training, and Normal
  Infant Sleep.* Amarillo: Praeclarus Press, 2014.

Middlemiss, Wendy. "Bringing the Parent Back into Decisions about Nighttime Care."
  Clinical Lactation. 4.2 (2013): 71-76.

Mindell, Jodi A., Brett Kuhn, Daniel S. Lewin, Lisa J. Meltzer, and Avi Sadeh. "Behavioral
  Treatment of Bedtime Problems and Night Wakings in Infants and Young
  Children." *Sleep* 29.10 (2006): 1263-1276.

Mirmiran, Majid, Yoland G. H. Mass, and Roland L. Ariagno. "Development of Fetal and
  Neonatal Sleep and Circadian Rhythms." *Sleep Medicine Reviews* 7.4 (2003):
  321-334.

Moon, Rachel, ed. *Sleep: What Every Parent Needs to Know.* Elk Grove Village: American
  Academy of Pediatrics, 2013.

Porgess, Stephen W., and Senta A. Furman. "The Early Development of the Autonomic Nervous System Provides a Neural Platform for Social Behavior: a Polyvagal Perspective." *Infant and Child Development* 20.1 (2011): 106-118.

Price, Anna M. H., Melissa Wake, Obioha C. Ukoumunne, and Harriet Hiscock. "Five-Year Follow-Up of Harms and Benefits of Behavioral Infant Sleep Intervention: Randomized Trial." *Pediatrics* 130.4 (2012): 643-651.

Ross, Lori E., Brian J. Murray, and Meir Steiner. "Sleep and Perinatal Mood Disorders: A Critical Review." *Journal of Neuroscience and Psychiatry* 30 (2005): 247-256.

Spencer, J. A. D., D. J. Moran, A. Lee, D. Talbert. "White Noise and Sleep Induction." *Archives of Diseases in Childhood* 65.1 (1990): 135-137.

Waldburger, Jennifer and Jill Spivak. *The SleepEasy Solution: The Exhausted Parent's Guide to Getting Your Child to Sleep From Birth to Age 5.* Deerfield Beach: HCI, 2007.

Weisbluth, Marc. *Healthy Sleep Habits, Happy Child.* New York: Random House, 1999.

West, Kim. *The Sleep Lady's Good Night, Sleep Tight: Gentle Proven Solutions to Help Your Child Sleep Well and Wake Up Happy.* New York: Vanguard Press, 2010.

How infant temperament affects sleep
(Best completed no earlier than 4-6 months, and will change over time depending on age and development)

	Much stimulation needed (not very sensitive)	Medium	Little stimulation needed (very sensitive)	
SENSITIVITY - The amount of stimulation (lights, sounds, touch) needed to produce a reaction in your infant.				Affects what baby needs in the sleeping environment: darkened room, white noise, visual stimulation, texture of fabrics, air temperature, scent.
GENERAL ACTIVITY - Your infant's level of physical activity (moving, kicking, waving arms) when sleeping, crying, lying in the crib, or reacting to child care procedures (diapering, dressing, bathing, feeding).	Low	Moderate	High	Affects baby's response to swaddling. May affect how their motor development progresses, and how much they need to practice new physical skills.
GENERAL INTENSITY - The intensity of your infant's expression of likes and dislikes in reaction to feedings, people, toys, or child care procedures.	Mild	Moderate	Intense	Affects baby's response to practice sessions. Can affect social and emotional milestones like separation anxiety.
FRUSTRATION TOLERANCE - The length of time your infant will keep at an activity (grasping objects, watching, eating).	Long periods	Variable	Short periods	Affects how long baby can practice new skills, like sleeping without swaddling, or tummy time.
ADAPTABILITY - The speed with which the infant adjusts to novelties, changes, transitions, or child care procedures.	Fast adjusting	Variable	Slow adjusting	Affects how well baby sleeps in differing sleep environments (child care vs home), as well as changing routines (no more pacifiers, etc). Affects how babies transition from one activity to the next (ie, going from play time to nap time)
REGULARITY - The consistency in the pattern of your infant's hunger, sleep, and activity cycles.	Fairly regular	Variable	Fairly irregular	Affects sleep schedules and patterns and how consistent bedtime and naps are.
SOOTHABILITY - How easily your infant can be distracted or calmed when fussing or crying.	Easily and quickly calmed	Variable	Hard or slow to calm	Affects baby's ability to learn to self-soothe, and how she calms herself during a practice session

AMMA
PARENTING CENTER

Base Skills Checklist: what to have in place by baby's first birthday

Base Skills are the foundation of good sleep habits in the family. They are:
1. **Understanding cues and cries.** Offer sleep when you see the earliest signs of fatigue. Trust cues, not clocks. A sleeping baby may cry out but picking her up at the first peep may prevent another sleep cycle (we call this a "Fake Wake").
2. **A sleep-friendly environment**: cool, dark, quiet, white noise machine, no night light (or red light for tasks), few distractions, followed by exposure to light upon waking.
3. **Practicing sleep independence**, including separating feeding from eating, sleeping on a flat motionless surface, and lying down drowsy but awake. Understand your baby's temperament and how it affects his sleep behavior, learning and acceptance of independence.
4. **Daily rhythms and rituals**. Follow your baby's natural inclination towards repetition and routines by having a nap routine, a bedtime routine, feeding routines and a daily pattern of life. Babies thrive on predictability. If the daytime isn't regular, try at least to have regular "bookends" to the day (wakeup and bedtime), within about a 30-minute window.
5. **Working with sleep associations.** Support your baby with sustainable sleep associations like white noise, aromatherapy, lovies, bedtime routines, etc. Gently phase out those that are too hard to sustain long term, or that are disrupting sleep instead of supporting it.

Your baby will go in and out of sleep organization. Inconsistency is your new consistency. When the Six Sleep Sinkers happen (teething, travel, illness, developmental milestones, growth spurts, and parental stress), a solid base of sleep skills will allow you to respond attentively to your baby's needs while still maintaining the fundamentals. Here is a checklist you can use as you establish a good set of Base Skills.

❏ We understand our baby's cues, and act on the earliest signs of sleep. The earliest signs of drowsiness are looking away, body movements stilling or stopping, red eyelids, and withdrawing attention. Yawning, eye rubbing, and other overt signs come *after* the earliest signs.

❏ We know the difference between a "Fake Wake" and real wakefulness. We wait to get our baby up until we know she is truly awake.

❏ We own a good white noise machine. We turn it on at bedtime and at the start of a nap, and We turn it off when we get the baby up from sleep. The volume is as loud as a shower, and the pitch is low and rumbly.

❏ Our baby's room is very dark at sleep times. We darken the room with light-blocking shades or curtains, keep the hall light off, and use no night light. When we do use a small light, it is very dim, or red. We avoid cool light tones at night, especially from electronic devices.

❏ The room temperature in our baby's room is cool, about 68 to 72 degrees.

❏ We have modified our baby's sleep environment to make her room as calming (and uninteresting!) as possible.

❏ We have stopped using swaddling products, or are phasing them out. Restrictive clothing is only used while our baby's body needs the support, or until rolling.

☐ Our baby sleeps lying flat, unless she is still struggling with reflux.

☐ Our baby is no longer dependent on motion for sleep.

☐ We are putting our baby to sleep while he's drowsy but still a bit awake.

☐ If a pacifier is disrupting sleep, we have phased it out.

☐ We are not letting our baby fall asleep at the breast or bottle.

☐ We are making efforts to learn our baby's temperament, and what is most successful for him. We're also learning how our own temperament affects our experience of sleep.

☐ We use a lovey or other transitional object for comfort. We include it in the bedtime routine, and leave it in the crib with the baby as soon as our doctor gives permission.

☐ We use aromatherapy as a sleep association.

☐ We understand the common "Sleep Sinkers": teething, travel, illness, developmental milestones, growth spurts, parental stress. We know these are not successful times to expect, or work on, good sleep. Even if our family is going through a Sleep Sinker, we continue to maintain a base of good sleep practices.

Daytime Sleep

☐ Our baby is spending no more than 2 to 4 hours awake at a time during the day. We are offering naps when we see drowsy signs. We go by the cues, not the clock.

☐ Our baby goes down for a morning nap within about 60-90 minutes of waking up for the day. We protect this morning nap.

☐ If our baby is taking a short "naplet" at the end of the afternoon, we are protecting it, and planning for bedtime within no longer than 90 minutes after waking.

☐ We are using a "sleep-friendly" environment for daytime sleep as well as at night.

Nighttime sleep

☐ We are putting our baby to bed at the just-right time of night. We go by cues, not clocks.

☐ We start our bedtime routine about *30 minutes before bedtime*. If bedtime is 7:00 pm, it means our baby is in bed, lights out at 7:00 pm, and we started the bedtime routine at 6:30.

☐ We start dimming household lights about 30 minutes before bedtime.

☐ We wind down physical play and activity about 30 minutes before bedtime.

☐ If our baby is easily excitable, we have put enough space between something stimulating (eating, bath, play) and bedtime.

☐ Our bedtime routine is short, consistent, and predictable.

☐ If our baby wakes up in the night, we are feeding only when we're sure he's hungry. If we suspect our baby could drop a feeding, we are starting to cut down the number of ounces or minutes. We're also trying to "front load" calories during the day by offering more nursing and bottling sessions.